Xenophobe's®
guide to the
CANADIANS

Vaughn Roste
Peter W. Wilson

D1431726

Xenophobe's Guides

Published by Xenophobe's® Guides

Telephone: +44 (0)20 7733 8585
E-mail: info@xenophobes.com
Web site: www.xenophobes.com

Published 2002
New edition 2009, 2012
Reprinted/updated 2004, 2006, 2007, 2009,
2011, 2012, 2013, 2014

Xenophobe's® Guides are revised on a regular basis
and suggestions for updates are welcome.

Editor – Catriona Tulloch Scott
Series Editor – Anne Tauté
Cover designer – Jim Wire and Vicki Towers
Printer – CPI/Antony Rowe, Wiltshire

Acknowledgment and thanks are given to
everyone who provided ideas for the map.

Vaughn Roste would like to dedicate this book to
Michele and Jacqueso at whose house in the Pyrenees
it was started; to Cyril, who introduced him to the series
but especially to his family – Rita, Darryl, and Erica Roste.

ePub ISBN: 9781908120151
Mobi ISBN: 9781908120168
Print ISBN: 9781906042257

Contents

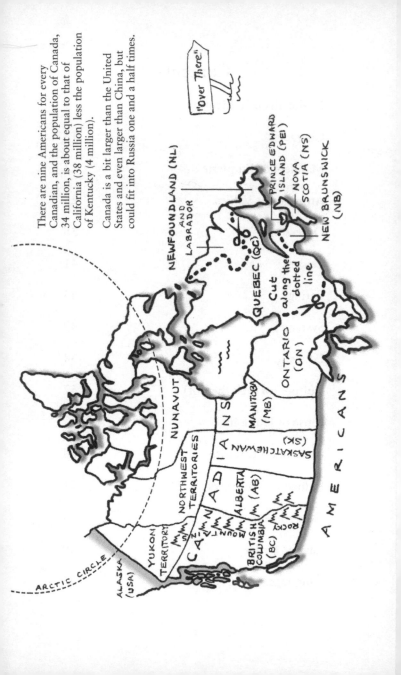

There are nine Americans for every Canadian, and the population of Canada, 34 million, is about equal to that of California (38 million) less the population of Kentucky (4 million).

Canada is a bit larger than the United States and even larger than China, but could fit into Russia one and a half times.

"Over There"

NEWFOUNDLAND (NL)
AND
LABRADOR

PRINCE EDWARD
ISLAND (PEI)

NOVA
SCOTIA (NS)

NEW BRUNSWICK
(NB)

QUEBEC (QC)

Cut along the dotted line

ONTARIO
(ON)

MANITOBA
(MB)

NUNAVUT

SASKATCHEWAN
(SK)

NORTHWEST
TERRITORIES

ALBERTA (AB)

C A N A D I A N S

YUKON
TERRITORY

ROCKY
MOUNTAINS

BRITISH
COLUMBIA
(BC)

A M E R I C A N S

ARCTIC CIRCLE

ALASKA
(USA)

Nationalism & Identity

Forewarned

Canadians are a disparate lot, their huge country created by volunteers from every other nation and consequently none too sure of just what it is itself.

The story is told of an early European explorer, Jacques Cartier, who asked the local natives what the area was called. They answered 'Kanata' and the term was subsequently applied to the northern half of the North American continent. Only later was it discovered that the word actually meant 'a small fishing village'.

Canada is the second largest country in the world (after Russia). Most other countries

> **Most other countries would fit several times into one Canadian province.**

would fit several times into one Canadian province. Its largest island, Baffin Island, is roughly twice as large as Great Britain (yet has only 28 settlements); there are national parks that are bigger than Switzerland; some of its lakes are larger than most seas – there's surf on a windy day on Lake Superior, for heaven's sake (though the most surfing that Canadians are ever likely to do is at home on the net).

Bordered by no less than three oceans, Canada is the country with the most coastline in the world. One glance at the northern islands and you will understand why. The nation doesn't have much coastline on the

Pacific side because the Americans somehow got away with buying Alaska from the Russians and thus laid claim to more than their fair share. But that's OK. Canadians are not resentful, and it turned out to be more of a liability in any case after the *Exxon Valdez* oil tanker had passed by.

Canada as a country is a conundrum. It is a savage land with gentle people, an enormous territory but sparsely populated, a wilderness at the forefront of technology, a culture defined as much or more by its regions as by any homogenous whole. Common ground comes with layers of protective clothing against -30°C of cold.

> **66 The nation doesn't have much coastline on the Pacific side because the Americans somehow got away with buying Alaska from the Russians. 99**

How they see themselves

To talk glibly of a Canadian identity is to conjecture, because this has yet to be firmly established. As one of Canada's poets sagely noted: 'It is only by our lack of ghosts that we are haunted.' The fact of the matter is that Canadians have no identity and are keenly seeking one. Canada's political bestsellers are often angst-ridden commentaries with titles such as *Canada on the World Stage: Is Anyone Listening?* and *The Future of Canada: Does Nationalism Even Matter?*

Much time and government funding has been spent in the public contemplation of the question of nationalism. One thing that everyone can agree on is that Canadians are NOT American. Any other statement made about Canadians pales in the face of this one.

Being NOT something else could be seen as the guiding principle around which the whole of Canadian society is based. (French Canadians have less of a difficulty with being NOT American, but are equally obsessed with protecting their identity and being NOT English Canadian, so the principle is the same.) Consequently, anything the Americans do Canadians are compelled to NOT do, even if they secretly envy the Americans for doing it.

> **66 One thing that everyone can agree on is that Canadians are NOT American. 99**

Americans seem to have staked a monopoly on patriotism (on the North American continent at least), which makes Canadians feel oddly uncomfortable about it. Canadians would be much more patriotic if they just didn't feel so American when they are.

That said, Canadians tend to be fiercely loyal to their own particular region: Atlantic Canada, Central Canada, Western Canada, and the North. To that you need to add an intense loyalty to tribe – French Canadians, British Canadians, Native Canadians and Métis (descendants of marriages between the earliest European settlers and the earliest inhabitants) who make up the largest and most easily identifiable groups, but don't tell that to the others. To name but a few, there are proud Italian Canadians (who claim that they 'built Toronto' – a slightly exaggerated but not totally inaccurate boast), Portuguese Canadians, Greek Canadians, Chinese Canadians (whose ancestors constructed huge sections of the Canadian Pacific trans-continental railway and whose Chinatowns in Toronto and Vancouver are the largest in North America), German Canadians, Indian Canadians, Ukrainian Canadians (who farmed the early-ripening wheat that led to Canada becoming 'the Granary of the World') – and, of course, Americans who seem to move to Canada in droves (particularly if there is a US war on).

> **66 With the price of cross-country flights taxed into the stratosphere, Canadians don't see much of each other. 99**

With the price of cross-country flights taxed into the stratosphere (it costs less to fly from Toronto to Prague than Vancouver), Canadians don't see much of each other. Some members of the older generation have never strayed far from the province of their birth. Only in recent decades has the populace become more mobile.

This has aggravated the already acute case of regionalism. 'Central' Canada, meaning Ontario and Quebec, is the most populous, and thus decides the bulk of the seats in federal elections. 'The West', defined as anything west of Ontario (when in fact Manitoba is geographically quite central), cries foul at every opportunity and complains constantly of being ignored and under-represented. The Atlantic provinces in the East would complain too – as would British Columbia at the other extreme – if only other Canadians would listen.

These geographical divisions do not begin to address the deeper linguistic and cultural ones. Quebec does not have the monopoly on French-speaking citizens but has appointed itself to speak for them anyway, so when French-speaking Manitobans or Ontarians or Maritimers (New Brunswick is completely bilingual) are not complaining that they are being mistreated, they feel they have grounds to complain that the Quebecois are interfering.

> **66 Albertans will tell you with a straight face how much like Texans they are, with their cattle ranches and oil wells. 99**

Whenever the global price of oil is high, Alberta (which oozes with it) starts grumbling about having to 'subsidize' the Eastern provinces. Albertans will tell you with a straight face how much like Texans they are, with their cattle ranches and oil wells. It seems not to register with them that the climates are some-what different, with the average Texas cow not having to spend the coldest nights of winter wrapped in a parka.

The British Columbians with their liberal attitudes would like to think of themselves as a northern extension of California. In Nova Scotia (at least outside the port of Halifax), they are too busy trying to bring back Scots Gaelic and arguing about the ruination of traditional fiddle tunes by modern performers to worry about less pressing concerns in other regions.

First Nation peoples (only the brazenly politically incorrect would still call them Red Indians) struggle for self-government within the confederation of Canada but it still remains a distant dream for most of them – a situation that has even been condemned by the United Nations. Self-government has, however, been largely achieved for Canada's Inuit (no longer called Eskimos). With the creation of the Territory of Nunavut in 1999, the Inuit were granted an unprecedented land claim in Canada: 26,500 people were given self-governing powers over an area roughly four times the size of France. Canadians elsewhere were by and large quite content with this decision. Not only was the land being returned to its original inhabitants, but it was a fairly painless process. The remainder of the population was frankly astounded that anyone would really want to live that far north.

> ❝In Nova Scotia they are too busy arguing about the ruination of traditional fiddle tunes to worry about less pressing concerns in other regions.❞

Sheer geography is the first formidable obstacle in getting Canadians to see each other at all – it takes over 100 hours just to cross the country one way by bus (not that many would consider doing so). This has led the Canadians to invent ways for some of its young people to see their own country. One programme, Katimavik, enabled willing teenagers to spend a year in three different demographically representative areas across the country. Such programmes are one of the few ways that Jason Oglukark from Whitehorse, Yukon, will ever find himself in the same room with Jessica Petersen from Bawlf (AB), Angela Chang of Agassiz (BC), Shane Hugotrimsky from Mozart (MB), Patrick McCormick of Moncton (NB), David Two Horses from Kenora (ON), or Marie-Claude Bourgeau from Rimouski (QC), let alone be friends. This is what ex-participant Will Ferguson had to say about his experience within one scheme: 'It's a purely Canadian programme: painfully well intentioned, resolutely optimistic, vaguely socialistic, very idealistic, and publicly funded. National brotherhood by bureaucratic mandate.'

Regionalism begets isolationism, so when visitors from another part of the country do come tramping through your neck of the woods, they may be wel-

> **Sheer geography is the first formidable obstacle in getting Canadians to see each other at all.**

comed or may not, depending on what preconceived ideas you might have formed about them from the media or Aunt Josephine's experience of them when she was there in '68.

It is the hard luck of the inhabitants of Newfoundland (semi-affectionately nicknamed 'Newfies') to be singled out for special attention. Because of their accent, and the fact that the rest of Canada secretly suspects them of being inbred, Newfies are the butt of merciless jokes.

> 66 Canada spreads across six time zones and Newfoundland is one half hour set off from the zones on either side. 99

Witness the Newfie old-timer who, talking about the sighting of beluga whales off the coast, exclaimed: 'There was t'ousands and t'ousands of 'em, maybe even hundreds!'

Newfoundland was a colony of Britain until 1949, and is thus Canada's newest province. A time zone has been created specially for it. Canada spreads across six time zones and Newfoundland is one half hour set off from the zones on either side. This makes it appear as if Newfies get their information 30 minutes behind everyone else and are always running to catch up. Television announcements which go Canada-wide have to accommodate the special time zone: 'The news tonight at seven, seven-thirty in Newfoundland...' The implication is that when the world ends, Newfies will be the last to know.

Special relationships

The Canadians maintain special relationships with the British and the French, the two founding nations that discovered their continent and settled its shores, all about 20,000 years after the indigenous peoples had already done the very same thing.

Because Canada is a constitutional monarchy the Canadians have close ties with Britain and the Commonwealth. Canada is also a major member of the *Francophonie* (France's answer to Britain's Commonwealth). However, most Canadians (French Canadians included) do not have a lot of warm fuzzy feelings for the former French Empire.

The Canadians' most special relationship, naturally, is with the Americans. Although reluctant to admit it, Canadians admire the free-wheeling

> 66 Although reluctant to admit it, Canadians admire the free-wheeling worldliness of their North American counterparts. 99

worldliness of their North American counterparts. Many have American origins or are married to Americans. Others have lived and worked in the U.S. for extended periods. Interestingly, almost 90% of Canada's population live within 300 kilometres of the American border. Can't live with them ... so they live near them. When the order is given for Canadians to invade the U.S., 30 million people are going to be across the border within three hours.

But it is a tenuous situation to be so perilously exposed to the world's only superpower. Former Prime Minister Pierre Trudeau compared it to being in bed with an elephant: one can sleep, but only very lightly. It is understandable therefore that Canadians have persistent and paranoid fears about being assimilated, culturally or worse, into the United States. One really LARGE 51st state.

❝ Living next door to the Americans has imbued Canadians with a natural sort of inferiority complex. ❞

Canada and the US share the longest undefended (in the military sense) border in the world. Until the post 9/11 American security paranoia, many small crossings along the frontier were actually unmanned. But, in a cultural sense, the border is rabidly defended. Niagara Falls (Ontario), and Niagara Falls (New York state) may be neighbouring cities, but they belong to separate nations. (The famous landmark is shared, but the awesome Horseshoe Falls belongs exclusively to the Canadians, so they definitely got the better half of that deal.)

Living next door to the Americans has imbued Canadians with a natural sort of inferiority complex. It's tough to prove that you are the worthier partner if your attention-seeking spouse continually steals the limelight, gladly takes the credit and bathes in all the glory afterwards. (Their neighbours to the north, over the Pole, are the Russians. This does little to ease the

Canadian sense of nervous inferiority.)

Canadians would love to get more attention, even if that recognition is not always in the most positive light. Hence they were more elated at their prominent role in the *South Park* hit 'Blame Canada' than upset at the ludicrous manner in which they were portrayed. It was reassuring to know that at least they were being noticed.

The French Connection

Though Newfoundlanders will point out that their capital, St. John's, was a bustling centre for trade decades before the French arrived, French Canadians feel they have the longest history in Canada and that in many ways Quebec *was* Canada.

> **French Canadians feel they have the longest history in Canada and that in many ways Quebec *was* Canada.**

After the British conquest, Quebec became a French-speaking colony in what was then British North America. The practice of their Roman Catholic religion was guaranteed by Britain, as was their language. Later, the American Revolution brought a torrent of refugees from the 'land of liberty', few of whom spoke French. Most subsequent immigrants tended also to be English speakers. English-only Canadians coming to Quebec expected to communicate in English, but French-only

Canadians could not go anywhere with the expectation of being able to communicate in French.

By the 1960s Quebecers had had enough and calls for separation began. Two referenda on the separation issue have been held, in 1980 and 1995, where the separatists obtained 40% and 49% of the vote in favour of divorcing from Canada. These referenda tend to be viewed by English Canadians as a Quebecois ploy to get more attention, but enviously so, because it works.

> **66 If one thing is obvious it is that the two lots of Canadians feel strongly about their weak attachments to each other. 99**

The Supreme Court of Canada has ruled that if a majority of any province gives a clear indication that they want independence, Canada as a country should not stop them. The populace waits to see if the French majority in Quebec will decide to put up with the rest of Canada, or if it thinks it worth the cultural and economic estrangement to break up.

Emotions on both sides of the debate are quite intense: if one thing is obvious it is that the two lots of Canadians feel strongly about their weak attachments to each other. Any movement in Quebec to separate is matched in fervour by the other regions saying how badly they want Quebec to stay in Canada. It is easy to see why: with the loss of Quebec goes the reason for all those years of painfully learning French.

How they see the rest of the world

Living in such a large country, the Canadians have a kind of 'Over There' perspective on anything that happens overseas. Europeans are treated with deference, but are definitely part of the Old World. Events 'over there' have little effect on day-to-day life 'over here'. They see overseas as somewhere very nice to visit, but can't really imagine any rational Canadian wanting to live there.

How others see them

Canadians travelling overseas are best advised to say they come from Toronto, Montreal or Vancouver, whether or not this is true. Nobody has ever heard of anywhere else and, if they have, they'll ask if you live near there and whether you know Jack. You will never get anywhere trying to describe where it is close to: nowhere in Canada is close to anywhere else.

> **66 You will never get anywhere trying to describe where it is close to: nowhere in Canada is close to anywhere else. 99**

Americans do not tend to view Canadians as being any different from themselves. If they do perceive any differences at all, these are mostly meteorological: cold fronts come 'down from Canada'. To Americans, Canadians are merely Americans inhabiting a colder part of the continent somewhere 'up there' in roughly the same place as Alaska. Al Capone reportedly said, 'Canada? I don't even know what street that's on.' (In fact he did know, since Canadians were smuggling lots of booze to him at the time.) Americans have all heard of Canada, but they seem to have missed the part of the lesson where it was specified that it was a separate and sovereign country.

> **66** Americans have all heard of Canada, but they seem to have missed the part of the lesson where it was specified that it was a separate country. **99**

However, they admit that Canadians sure know how to play hockey and have somehow figured out how to make better beer, though for some inexplicable reason Americans seem to harbour a nagging suspicion that all Canadians are born with the instinctive knowledge of how to gut a bear.

The French, seemingly still somewhat bitter that things didn't quite go according to plan in the war (that's the Seven Years War of 1756–1763 featuring Generals Wolfe and Montcalm and the walled city of Quebec), are always keen to welcome Canadians back from the colonies – and show them around civilisation. They view French Canadians as siblings, and are disconcerted to discover that there are some Canadians (about 40%) who cannot speak any French at all.

European stereotypes of Canadians are much more flattering. They remember Canadians kindly from their heavy involvement in past wars and even former enemies seem to have no hard feelings. The Dutch have a particular bond. Every May millions of tulips bloom along the canal built in the nation's capital – a breathtakingly beautiful gift from the people of Holland as thanks for granting safety

> **The rest of the world sees Canadians as a tough, undomesticated people... heroically pushing back the barriers of the known world.**

to the exiled Dutch Royal Family in WWII. (Princess Margriet was born in Ottawa as a result.)

The rest of the world sees Canadians as a tough, undomesticated people hacking life out of a frozen landscape and heroically pushing back the barriers of the known world.

How they would like to be seen

Canadians would like to be seen as world peace makers, rugged pioneers, industrious workers, accomplished outdoorsmen, good and gracious conquerors of their savage land and a homogenous tribe of *savoir-faire* environmentalists. They consider that their bilingualism means they are the enlightened half, and redeeming grace, of North American society.

But Canadians are grounded in reality. A competition run by a radio show asked readers to complete a sentence that began 'As Canadian as ...'. The winning entry was: 'As Canadian as possible under the circumstances.'

Character

Qualities forged by nature

Two things define Canadians more than anything else: weather and geography.

Weather in Canada is remarkably easy to predict. It is either: a) incredibly cold; b) incredibly cold with severe weather warnings; c) brutally hot; d) brutally hot with severe weather warnings; e) windy. There is very little in between.

Winter frequently turns to summer in a matter of weeks, the number of weeks being scientifically determined across Canada by a series of groundhogs who appear out of their holes on 2nd February. If they spot their shadow, they scoot back into their dens and hibernate for another six weeks. Ontario is home to a famous groundhog, Wiarton Willie, who has his own statue. When he died aged 22 in the winter of 1998-99, a funeral was held for him as people said they needed closure. In fact it doesn't matter whether the groundhogs see shadows on Groundhog Day or not – there are always six more weeks of winter.

'If some countries have too much history, Canada has too much geography,' said former Prime Minister

William Lyon Mackenzie King. Having so much land has a great effect on the character, customs and culture of the nation. Take, for example, the prairies. The plains of Canada stretch out endlessly. The flattest spot in the world can be found here, with nary a tree to obstruct the view, which leaves the prairie observer with a remarkably huge view of nothing. In Saskatchewan, people say that you can watch your dog running away for three days.

It has been said that three dimensions govern the prairies: the sky, the land, and the loneliness. The sheer physical fact of the prairie has produced two opposite states of mind: 'man, the giant-conqueror, and man, the insignificant dwarf always threatened by defeat'. This paradox has led Canadians to define themselves as simultaneously omnipotent and puny.

Taming a savage wasteland can give anyone a feeling of omnipotence. Thus fearlessness characterizes many Canadians' behaviour. They will say, 'I can

66 Ontario is home to a famous groundhog, Wiarton Willie. When he died a funeral was held as people said they needed closure. **99**

do anything', with a sense of imperviousness and impunity. But gaping up at the Canadian Rockies or sailing a fishing boat home in a 30-foot swell, you are dwarfed by the sheer magnitude of your surroundings, and compared with almighty Nature, you can quickly begin to feel rather insignificant.

The Canadian Shield is another place that has this effect. Thought to have been so named because it does indeed provide a natural defence, this is an enormous area not only rich in mineral resources but marked by beautiful forested vistas, big boulders, shady pines, cool tranquil waters, soothing moss-covered rocks, ripple-less lakes, more forests, more enormous rocks,

> **❝ Canadians have developed a refined nonchalance about travelling great distances. ❞**

more lakes, more trees... The Shield keeps throwing them at you until you're desperate for a change. The immensity of this region never fails to impress, especially those who are still trying to get out. Experiences like this go a long way towards making one unpretentious.

Canadians have developed a refined nonchalance about great distances, and every family dreams of one day driving across the country. Sitting in a vehicle for incredible durations would strike most Europeans as masochistic, but Canadians display a perverse sort of pleasure in it, and an immunity that comes with exposure: some Canadians commute ten hours to work.

True Grit

Canadian winters can be daunting to the uninitiated, and the summers can be equally intimidating. This affects the mind-set of its people: you tend to get used to adapting to extremes.

In the north, the earth is all tundra, the name for ground that never completely thaws out, even in summer when, despite the sun blazing away 24 hours a day, the ground only thaws to a depth of a few centimetres. Consequently trees only attain a diminutive height. It is a phenomenon when travelling north on a Canadian highway to watch the trees grow shorter and shorter. Who needs drugs?

Inhabitants of the Territories in the far north are unimpressed by anything less than gale force winds and a wind chill of -55°C. But it takes a lot of personal motivation to get out of bed on sub-zero mornings when, as the expression goes, 'it's so cold you have to back up to pee' (in theory, keeping moving stops you from getting glued to the ground).

> **It takes a lot of personal motivation to get out of bed on sub-zero mornings when, as the expression goes, 'it's so cold you have to back up to pee.'**

Where things are this cold, the pace of life can vary greatly, from leisurely to glaciatic. It takes time to get your order flown in or to get that necessary spare part for a broken-down machine; it also takes time for the ice to melt, and it takes a long time to get anywhere else. Even vegetation grows so slowly that cart tracks left by Sir Edward Parry's 1820 expedition were still visible 158 years later. Many northern communities are dependent on bush planes, small aircraft that have modified landing gear so that they can use Canada's myriad lakes as runways. In Dawson (Yukon) in winter, each home has to bleed litres of warmed water every hour into the sewers to keep them from freezing up.

Living in the extreme north can be depressing. Many buildings are windowless for reasons of insulation, and time spent outdoors in winter is necessarily minimal. The population is too small to ensure much social interaction. The suicide rate amongst Canada's Inuit is reported to be six times higher than the national average. One needs to be emotionally hardy merely to survive.

66 In the middle of the worst possible ice storm, someone will still manage to say: 'Well, at least there's no flies out today.' 99

Canadians wear an austere smile in the face of adversity, and have a 'grin and bear it' mentality, even if the grin is frozen on their faces by the cold. In the middle of the worst possible ice storm, someone will still manage to say: 'Well, at least there's no flies out today.'

The Canadian attitude to the cold is an admirable show of good faith – mostly in the down filling of one's parka. Canadians tend to look down on anyone who says he can't handle the cold, and like to think that extreme weather conditions build character. Having survived two weeks of -35°C, all of a sudden -10°C is a summer day. Canadians break out the deckchairs and start sunning themselves. The wearing of shorts on spring days that are warmer than their winter counterparts but are still technically freezing is indulged in mostly by foolhardy young students referred to as 'cooligans'.

Summers by contrast can be brutally hot (30°–40°C) with unrelenting steamy humidity – particularly in Ontario and Quebec. This

> **66 Canadians like to think that extreme weather conditions build character. 99**

often creates dangerous thunder storms (more properly lightning storms). Despite the warnings on local radio, dozens are killed every year by lightning.

Canadians admire a 'stick-to-it' attitude that can be driven by inspiration, perspiration, or something that borders on the insane. Terry Fox, who had a leg amputated due to cancer, ran across the country to raise money for cancer research and won the hearts of a generation of Canadians, many of whom still retain a mental image of the young man battling through heat, rain and snowstorms along the Trans-Canada highway. Thousands participate in the annual fund-raising run named after him, known as the Marathon of Hope.

Not all Canadians are this tough. In the evening of life, accustomed to finer pleasures, many succumb to a distinctly Canadian phenomenon – they become snowbirds. These are wealthy older Canadian couples who, bird-brained or not, migrate south year after year to winter in warmer climes, leaving someone else in charge of shovelling the walk. There are suburbs in Florida and Hawaii composed entirely of Canadians who stay until the first spring breeze sends them home again. Naturally, they would never consider emigration. Even those who live in the sun all year round keep a Canadian address so that they can ensure their health care benefits don't lapse.

Manners & Etiquette

The Canadian climate has ramifications for Canadian buildings and behaviour. For instance, many homes have an entrance with two doors, an outer and an inner, to help keep costly warmth from escaping. There has to be a place for storing boots, gloves, hats and jackets and adding or subtracting multiple layers of warm clothes.

The climate has imposed on the populace the habit of putting on a jacket when going outside regardless of how warm or cold it is: the season merely determines the weight of the jacket, not its presence or absence. It is customary to remove one's boots or shoes at the entrance. Not to do so is a sign of disrespect: one does not tramp snow through the house. This practice is continued in summer even when there isn't any snow.

Politeness personified

Canadians are noted for being exceptionally polite. They find it shocking that the English can ask: 'How do you do?' and then turn away without waiting to hear the reply. If you really don't care to know, you ought not to ask.

A Canadian is quick to apologize even when it is you who inadvertently bumped him in the street. Both parties tend to thank each other at the end of a telephone conversation. If you dump four weeks' worth of work on someone unexpectedly, he will thank you for having stopped by. Bank tellers will thank you for your business. Motorists often automatically thank the cop who is giving them a speeding ticket. People will often hold a door open for you and not just if you are female. Pedestrians in smaller towns have to take care not even to look as if they would like to cross the street (regardless of corner or intersection) since cars are likely to stop and wait for them.

❝ Pedestrians in smaller towns have to take care not even to look as if they would like to cross the street since cars are likely to stop and wait for them. ❞

A woman suffering from amnesia was discovered aimlessly wandering the streets of Los Angeles. Police had only one clue as to her identity: she was polite. So polite, in fact, they figured she had to be Canadian. Sure enough, when an all points bulletin went out across Canada, it turned out she was. Politeness is clearly so ingrained in the Canadian psyche that one will still remember to be polite even after forgetting who one is.

There is a limit to all this gallantry, however. In one area the rules of polite society no longer apply. As soon as Canadians strap on skates, all common decency and respect for others is thrown right out of the window, particularly for anyone not wearing the same colour jersey.

> **66 As soon as Canadians strap on skates, all respect for others is thrown right out of the window. 99**

Canadians are notoriously bad tippers. If the service was especially good, you might squeeze 10% out of them. If not, they may not tip at all. Hence the sight of hotel and restaurant staff falling over themselves in unseemly haste to serve American tourists. It's not necessarily because they love Americans, it's just that they're bigger tippers.

'Eh?'

'Eh?', which has become a Canadian trademark, is defined in a dictionary as 'ascertaining the continued interest and comprehension of the listener'.

Not giving offence is thought to be the underlying reason for Canadians adding this interrogative to the end of a sentence. They can thus subtly transform an assertion into a hypothesis. Following some statement with an 'eh?' places a bit of verbal distance after whatever possibly offensive comment the speaker may have made, and makes it just a little more likely that the listener will forgive whatever it was that might have upset him in the first place.

Attitudes & Values

Multi-culturalism

Lacking even a common language to unify the populace, there is no obvious universal national characteristic one can use to rally the people. But instead of treating this absence as something that needs to be overcome, Canadians have decided that differences are something that they will not only accept, but actively embrace, promote and celebrate.

According to one Canadian sociologist, 'Canada has decided to enshrine a demographic reality into a national virtue'. This attitude has been credited with helping Canada avoid the overt racism and gross economic disparities of other industrialized nations.

> **❝ Canadians have decided that differences are something that they will not only accept, but actively embrace, promote and celebrate. ❞**

Canadians coined the term 'multi-cultural' not as an act of creativity but necessity. It is thus official policy that the nation aspires towards a 'cultural mosaic', something like a patchwork quilt, whereas Americans have aimed for a 'melting pot'. Canadians are essentially practical, and have figured out that the bat-brained idea of a melting pot would not work in a country where 50% of the land never completely thaws at all. A quilt is a much more pragmatic idea: it's cold outside.

A sense of decency

In the settling of the Canadian provinces, the early pioneers had no-one to rely on but themselves and their near neighbours. In such circumstances you learned that you needed each other in times of difficulty, and that people were more likely to lend you a tool if you returned it.

> **The nation aspires towards a 'cultural mosaic', something like a patchwork quilt, whereas Americans have aimed for a 'melting pot'.**

Honesty and integrity were important, not to mention things like a good reputation and a virtuous character. It's an attitude that persists to this day. In areas with a sparse population, one cannot underestimate the power of public opinion: peer pressure promotes public propriety. The story is told of a Canadian who walked into a drugstore intent on robbery. After patiently waiting his turn in line, he found he'd

26

forgotten his weapon, so he informed the pharmacist that he would be back in half an hour to complete the heist. The police, on hand to arrest him later, commented that not only did he keep his word, he was even punctual.

Tolerance

Early settlers quickly learned to overlook their neighbour's personal quirks and eccentricities. It's a mental extension of dealing with the weather: if you know you cannot change it, you might as well accept it.

Thus, the Canadian electorate puts up with incredibly unpopular decisions, policies and leaders mostly because they figure that trying to change the system is about 'as useless as pyjamas on a bride'. It has been suggested that the extent of Canadian tolerance and compromise can be deduced from the mere fact that Canada continues to exist. However, the amount of tolerance in Canada could end up being the death of it too. Tolerance is valued to such an extent that political leaders dedicated to the dissolution of the country are sworn into public office despite being members of separatist federal parties.

> **❝ The electorate puts up with unpopular decisions...they figure that trying to change the system is about 'as useless as pyjamas on a bride'. ❞**

Canada is the first nation to have created a Charter of Rights and Freedoms making illegal all discrimination on grounds of race, religion, sex or sexual orientation. It is also the nation that conceived Greenpeace, and gave the world Harlequin Romance (Mills & Boon).

Canadians have been described as 'gradualists' because their social transformations tend to be more gradual than precipitous. They don't have a history of change through violence so don't like revolt or upheaval of any sort. Nor do they like guns: they live by peace-keeping, not policing. During the Suez Crisis in 1956 when Canada's Foreign Affairs Minister Lester B. Pearson proposed a peace-keeping mission to try to avert a war, he initiated what would come to be defined as one of Canada's most respected and major roles. Whereas the American constitution ensures 'life, liberty, and the pursuit of happiness,' its Canadian counterpart promises 'peace, order, and good government' – though many Canadians see 'good government' as a contradiction in terms. Failing that, they'd happily settle for peace and order.

> **❝This is the nation that conceived Greenpeace, and gave the world Harlequin Romance (Mills & Boon).❞**

Lack of pretension
Canadians are down-to-earth, even earthy, people.

They keep each other that way. Arrogance is curtailed by a lack of things about which to brag, although in your presence a Canadian might have caught a larger fish or climbed a higher mountain than you have, and killed a more ferocious grizzly bear (with his bare hands, naturally).

People from British Columbia are a bit conceited about their climate, thinking somehow that every nice day in Canada should belong to them, and Western Canadians once having seen the Rockies are likely to call anything less than 5,000 feet a hill. Other than that, Canadians are pretty easy to get along with. Just don't ask them what part of 'the States' they're from.

The Canadian attitude towards wealth might best be illustrated by how Canadian lottery winners spend their money. While US or UK lotto winners are apt to buy the

66 Western Canadians once having seen the Rockies are likely to call anything less than 5,000 feet a hill. 99

house and car of their dreams to show off to the neighbours, Canadians are more likely to take off on a trip. Canadian wealth is exhibited rather discreetly by the amount of time that one is not at home. This leads to a 'they're not home again, they must be doing all right for themselves' reaction. It's an example of post-modern Canadian mentality – the flaunting of riches by their noticeable absence. It's so much more polite.

29

Natural concerns

Canadians love the great outdoors – 20% of Canadians go camping each year – and consider the natural phenomena of their country to be unequalled in the world. More than 90% of Canada remains undeveloped, and Canadians would like to keep it that way. But it's a worry. Not all Canadians have seen the Rockies, but every single one of them wants them to be well cared for and not buried by commercial developments or tourist litter or raped by a strip-mine by the time they get there. The rate of replanting trees now exceeds the rate of cutting them down, which ultimately merely ensures sufficient nourishment for the spruce pine beetle.

> **66 Residents of Churchill, Manitoba, would be surprised if they didn't see bears ambling nonchalantly through their streets each year. 99**

Hunting, which requires a permit, is for most folk more of an exercise in male bonding as father-and-son-go-for-a-walk-in-the-woods-carrying-guns-but-don't-see-anything. Animal rights activists protest loudly against trapping and shooting animals for any reason other than self-defence. Only First Nations have a right to hunt year-round to make up for the loss of their traditional lifestyles. Banff National Park has constructed the world's first highway overpass reserved exclusively for wild animals, and they use it. Residents of Churchill, Manitoba, would be surprised if they didn't see bears ambling nonchalantly through their streets each year as everyone is aware that the city sits plumb in the middle of their migratory routes.

Because landfill sites no longer provide satisfactory solutions to the ever-present trash problem, several cities are using technology to transform household waste into soil-enriching compost. Edmonton has constructed North America's biggest composter. Citizens place recyclable materials into blue bags which are picked up like regular garbage and taken to a sorting and treatment facility. The $100-million plant, which covers an area the size of four football fields, processes over 1,000 tonnes of refuse a day, enabling Edmonton to re-use 70% of its residential waste. Everything is recycled – from glass and cardboard milk cartons to metals, plastics and even concrete and asphalt from sidewalk repairs.

> 66 Everything, is recycled, from glass and cartons to concrete and asphalt from sidewalk repairs. 99

Another leader in recycling technology is Halifax where the recycling programme has made its way into law, making it illegal to throw an apple core into a garbage can.

Three's a crowd

The Canadians' concept of space has contributed to their sprawling metropolises. With no lack of land, their cities tend to grow horizontally rather than vertically. Just about every house in the suburbs has a large grassy lawn that requires mowing in summer and at least four trees: two at the front and two at the back. Vegetable gardens are optional. Add the municipally maintained trees that line the streets and you have towns occupying veritable forests. Aerial photographs of some urban areas are only distinguishable from areas of uninhabited woodlands by the odd four- or more storey building.

> **Canadians have their own version of personal space. There are those who begin to feel claustrophobic when more than four people gather together in a large room.**

There is no lack of breathing space inside most homes either. Canadian parents keep their multi-bedroomed homes long after the 2.3 children have left to create families of their own. It would be unthinkable not to have space for the family to stay when they all come home for the holidays, even with grandchildren in tow.

Living in one of the least densely populated countries in the world, Canadians have their own version of personal space. An outsider might see three people per square kilometre as immensely under-populated, but there are those who begin to feel claustrophobic when more than four people gather together in a large room. Therefore, as a general rule it may be best not to advance closer than one metre to a Canadian –

unless you intend getting more intimate.

Once a friendship has been established, people are not above giving hugs (kisses in Quebec), even man to man when the situation permits. But once the physical embrace is concluded Canadians return to their conventional distance, which is to say only close enough that one does not have to shout in order to be heard.

A host of religions

Canada has a long-standing policy of religious freedom (enshrined in its Charter of Human Rights and Freedoms). According to income tax regulations, you only need eight people to form a group to be legally recognised as a church, to which you may then make tax-deductible donations.

It was not always thus, as Jesuit missionary Jean de Brébeuf and his brethren discovered amongst the Hurons at Sainte Marie. It seems that the natives didn't think it right to give up their own religion and

> **"You only need eight people to form a group to be legally recognised as a church, to which you may then make tax-deductible donations."**

things got nasty. Not all was lost though, as Canada got its first beatified martyrs, and the hauntingly beautiful Huron Carol.

Many villages are peppered with churches all with serious, if few, adherents. The more 'evangelical' the church, the larger the congregation. It is not uncommon to find competing Christian churches – Roman Catholic, Baptist, Lutheran, Pentecostal, Anglican and United (a uniquely Canadian combination of Methodist, Presbyterian and Congregationalist) – in a town of no more than 5,000 people. In Quebec, the Roman Catholic Church has historically held powerful sway, while the North, the First Nations and large chunks of Ontario and the Maritimes are heavily Anglican.

> 66 Religious freedom has of late been taken as a freedom to not attend whatever denomination one chooses to call oneself. 99

More recent immigration has brought Hindus, Muslims, Buddhists, New Agers, Animists and staunch non-believers to Canadian society.

Religious freedom has of late been taken as a freedom to not attend whatever denomination one chooses to call oneself. Many Christian Canadians are found in church only at Christmas or for weddings. Even funerals are often now relegated to the funeral home 'chapel' or the parlour.

Religious studies are popular at university: alongside Western Christianity, dispassionate atheism (or apathetic agnosticism) characterizes the modern perspective. Tolerance, noted Canadian virtue that it is, can sometimes be elevated to the status of a religion.

34

Drinking distinctions

Attitudes to alcohol vary from province to province, not only on the legal drinking age but also on how late the bars stay open, where and by whom alcohol can be sold (in some places, spirits are available only in government-operated stores), and how much it is taxed. In Quebec not drinking is tantamount to blasphemy. In Ontario one must be 19 to drink, so 18-year-olds take regular excursions across the border into neighbouring Quebec, supposedly to improve their French but really to take advantage of the looser liquor laws.

❝ The popularity of distinctively Canadian beer and Canadian rye whisky makes them almost a unifying factor. ❞

A fair number of Canadians do not drink at all. Puritanism is strong in some rural areas, and self-imposed abstinence is common. This is especially true in the Prairie provinces, which, because of the simplicity of life and the communal emphasis on a religious upbringing, have been dubbed the Canadian Bible Belt (largely synonymous with the grain belt).

Across Canada, however, the popularity of distinctively Canadian beer and Canadian rye whisky makes them almost a unifying factor. Rye whisky is usually mixed (what Canadians call 'pressed') with coke or ginger ale. Rye whisky and water pressed with coke is especially popular in the West.

Canadian wines are difficult to obtain outside the

country, but are increasingly popular – particularly, but not exclusively, British Columbian and Niagara region whites. Some have actually won prestigious awards in France – much to the annoyance of the French.

Marriage

About a third of Canadian marriages end in divorce, a figure that has led many young Canadians to ratio-nalise that it is not worth the trouble of getting married in the first place, so they skip that step and start living together. One third of children in Canada are cur-rently born to parents who are co-habiting but unmarried, and single parent families are also very common. Others form blended families: couples today are just as likely to have to distinguish 'his' children from 'her' children as from the children they have had together.

> **Perpetually striving for amicable solutions to boost the population, the government offers monthly payments to families for each child.**

Perpetually striving for amicable solutions to boost the population, the government offers monthly pay-ments to families for each child until they reach 18. Studies have been inconclusive about the effectiveness of this 'baby bonus'; for instance, it is not known how many children in Canada would not have been produced otherwise. In Canada it seems the population needs federal and financial encouragement to make love.

The older generation

'The prime of life' is when many retired Canadians look forward to days spent actively pursuing those goals they never quite had the chance to achieve, especially sinking a hole-in-one.

Patching together the last square on the church quilt, finishing a 1,000-piece double-sided jigsaw puzzle or waiting your number in a bingo parlour is where the excitement is to be found. That is, outside the summers when the highways to Jasper and Banff are packed with bold retired couples roughing it in brand-new, 37-foot motor homes with more square footage than the average Parisian apartment. However, once they no longer wish to maintain their own homes, many ship themselves off to places where paid professionals take care of them.

> **❝ The highways to Jasper and Banff are packed with bold retired couples roughing it in brand-new, 37-foot motor homes. ❞**

By and large the older generation in Canada is accorded a lot of respect for having worked so hard to build the country and fought to keep it free – so long as they're not driving slowly in the left-hand (or worse, the only) lane.

Obsessions

Hockey

All sports pale in comparison with hockey, the sacred cow of Canadian sport. Even adding 'ice' before the word hockey is superfluous. Hockey is not the most important thing in life, hockey *is* life.

For those who do not understand the game, the circular black object that is batted around is actually irrelevant. Hockey is more akin to Team Boxing With Sticks. Due to its universal popularity (rare is the boy who does not learn to skate), hockey has been recognized as Canada's official winter sport, but only since 1994.

> **66 Hockey is not the most important thing in life, hockey *is* life. 99**

Canada's official summer sport is lacrosse, a game with Native North American origins and which most Canadians have never even seen, let alone played. They have a vague notion that lacrosse is something like the game of polo minus the horses.

The weekly televised *Hockey Night in Canada* is so well known that its opening tune is effectively the unofficial national anthem. Every Canadian boy dreams of being a professional hockey player and of one day making it to the National Hockey League. Those dreams are often still active when the boys have metamorphosed into middle-aged couch potatoes who can barely complete a successful manoeuvre to the fridge, far less 'deke out' (use a dummy shot to trick) the defenceman.

To make the grade and get accepted into the NHL is to be deified in Canada, as epitomised by billboards erected in a player's home town to boast the fact that 'Joey Canuck comes from here!'

No visitor to Canada should arrive without a minimal foreknowledge of Canadian hockey giants, such as Wayne Gretzky, Maurice 'Rocket' Richard, and Paul Henderson. Gretzky (a.k.a. 'the Great One') has freeways named after him on both sides of the country. Each spring the playoffs garner more attention than any other news item, and on the night of the

> **66 To make the grade and get accepted into the NHL is to be deified in Canada. 99**

NHL final, the country comes to a standstill. The first team to win four games receives the coveted Stanley Cup, and should the series (i.e., tournament) run to a seventh game, the entire country will hold its breath. If you are one of the few who aren't interested you will have an easy time driving on the streets that night, unless the game ends and you are in the city that has just won. In that case, beware the downtown core. Canadians, braving any weather, will be out celebrating with 100,000 of their very closest friends.

A mere hundred years ago, when the West was being settled, the Canadian government granted land cheaply or even free to those who would clear it.

When communities were being established and frontier towns built, the church was invariably the first building to be constructed (it served as school, courthouse, community centre and city hall), after which came the store and the grain elevator. Then came the ice rink. Every village in Canada down to the smallest hamlet, even if too small to have a school or field a team of same sized kids, has its own ice rink. It's a matter of necessity.

> 66 Every village in Canada down to the smallest hamlet, even if too small to have a school or field a team of same sized kids, has its own ice rink. 99

The maple leaf

Many Canadian travellers overseas sport decorative maple leaf pins on jackets and backpacks in the fond belief that it will identify them as NOT Americans. It doesn't: the moment they open their mouths only a fellow Canadian can tell the difference. But this does not deter them. True grit.

Even the Quebecois, who would never be caught dead with a Canadian symbol within the province of Quebec, have been known to switch allegiance when they leave the country and become some of Canada's most patriotic citizens, decking themselves in red and white (well, there are maple trees in Quebec, *n'est ce pas?*).

When American Marines mistakenly carried the Canadian flag upside down into a World Series baseball game, a cartoon in a Canadian national daily lampooned the famous image of American soldiers on Iwo Jima by showing them hoisting the Canadian flag – the wrong way up of course – while a sergeant behind them read the instruction manual. The caption read: 'Whoops.' T-shirts sprouted like magic bearing an upside-down Stars and Stripes emblazoned 'Sorry, eh?'

Canadians have been heard to claim that the Canadian flag is the most popular flag in the world. Why? Because it has a bar at each end.

Leisure

Canadians can feel a bit lost if they don't have major activities planned for the morning, afternoon and evening of each day, and the resulting clash in families trying to manage four or more hectic schedules is enough to burn out several high powered computers.

There's no sports like snow sports

Blessed with such an abundance of snow, Canadians have invented, learned or perfected everything there is to do on, around, to, in, with or under it. The children take sledges, toboggans, trays, even cardboard boxes, and spend hours happily running up hills so that they can slide down them again. Playing in the snow involves making snowmen, snowwomen (don't ask), complete snow families and snow forts, having snowball fights, and being snow angels by lying flat on your back in the snow and waving your arms about. Many graduate to skiing (both cross country and downhill), and for the truly obsessed who cannot wait until spring, there is snow golf, where you hit coloured balls around on top of packed snow.

Skidoos, massively popular as recreational vehicles, are vital for getting around in Canada's north. Said to have been invented when Joseph-Armand Bombardier had no means to get his sick child to the nearest hospital, they run on belts instead of wheels, enabling them to fly over snow-covered ground with adrenalizing power. There is scarcely a Canadian who would not recognize either the ladder-like track left by a skidoo or the characteristic whine of souped-up engines that disrupt many a peaceful Sunday afternoon.

66 There is scarcely a Canadian who would not recognize the ladder-like track left by a skidoo. 99

Curling, introduced to Canada by its Scottish immigrants, is a true passion: 94% of the world's players live in Canada.

Canadians have figured out that anything that can

be done on water can also be done on ice. There is ice fishing, ice sailing, ice racing on motorbikes with spiked metal tyres, and ice climbing (frozen waterfalls are great practice for glaciers and a challenge in themselves). The centrepiece of Quebec's annual Winter Festival is an exhibition of ice sculpting that attracts artists worldwide.

> **" Canadians have figured out that anything that can be done on water can also be done on ice. "**

Canadians have even incorporated the ubiquitous white stuff into their cuisine. In Quebec a favourite winter treat is made by taking hot maple syrup and pouring it over snow which freezes it instantly and makes an interesting taffy texture. Eating maple syrup and snow, what could be more Canadian than that?

Out at the lake

Canada has a huge number of lakes (Manitoba, for example, has one lake for every ten people) and many families own a small holiday cottage or cabin usually in close proximity to a lake where they can enjoy waterskiing, windsurfing, canoeing, kayaking, sailing, motor boat racing, and just hanging around near the lake shore. Some people have even been known to enter the water without the aid of a mechanical device just to go swimming.

Lake activities are not restricted to the summer months. Many folk fish in winter, which has the advantage of not needing a boat. Simply cut a hole in the frozen waters, take a seat and settle in for hours of enjoyment. Should the temperature be too cold, you can always set up a small heated shack which hopefully will take the bite out of the air, but not too big a bite out of the ice it's standing on.

> **Many folk fish in winter, which has the advantage of not needing a boat.**

Nor is swimming entirely out of the question. In the dead of winter a group known as the Polar Bear Club erect shelters on the ice, then cut holes in it and dive into the sub-zero water for the joy of running around in the snow afterwards before racing for the comfort of the glowing warm sauna. This is considered fun, or purging, although purging of what is not entirely clear – their senses is one possibility.

Summer camp and bush parties

A rite of passage in many an adolescent's life is summer camp. Unlike the American system where youngsters are sent away for the entire summer, Canadian camps tend to operate on a weekly basis. Nonetheless, Canadian parents avidly support the developmental rituals that summer camps provide, particularly the opportunity for parents to take a vacation on their own without the kids (sometimes second honeymoons that occur in their own house).

The rural equivalent of the urban house party when your parents are away is the Friday night bush party, when a bonfire is built in the middle of nowhere, large enough to attract attention, but not so huge that the wrong people turn up – like the police. It is sometimes the police who unwittingly provide the

❝As the true hub of Canadian society, the indoor mall is rivalled only by the doughnut store.❞

best advertisement for these events by arriving with their 'party lights' flashing: the size of the police entourage alerts those who are not already there to the scope of the event they are missing.

Malls

Canada has, of necessity, invented the indoor shopping mall. West Edmonton Mall, the world's largest temple to consumerism, is equivalent in size to 48 city blocks. Malls are not just the place to shop but also a common meeting point, a social occasion, an amicable outing. As the true hub of Canadian society, the indoor mall is rivalled only by the doughnut store.

Downtown buildings of many Canadian cities are connected by underground tunnels or second-storey skywalks, allowing you to stroll about in comfort getting everything you need without ever having to brave the outdoors. And, in the depth of winter, with amenities such as remote car starters and automatic garage door openers Suzy Shopper can make her purchases, drive back to suburbia and step directly into her centrally heated home, all without ever once having to set foot outside.

Eating

You will rarely be offered more choice of food than in Canada – from the Yorkshire Pudding beloved of the British Canadians, and sugar pies traditional to the Quebecois, to the sauerkraut and sushi of its multifarious inhabitants. Each region also has its own dishes: Pacific salmon in the West, Alberta beef, First Nations' bannock. Cod is a favourite in Newfoundland, sourdough bread is popular in the Yukon, while Prince Edward Island is famed for its red potatoes. Beaver tails (fried, flattened dough in the shape of a beaver's tail, covered with sugar and cinnamon) delight children; moose burgers are generally reserved for tourists.

66 Beaver tails (fried, flattened dough covered with sugar and cinnamon) delight children. 99

Canadians insist on a quality that few other nations could possibly afford. The earliest pioneers learned to make delicious meals from what was fresh and in season. Nowhere is this more evident than in French Canada, where you can sample mouth-watering homemade casseroles, tender roasts, *bouillabaisse*, *cipaille*s and *tortières* (meat pies), game birds, venison, *fèves au lard* (beans and bacon), soufflés, soups, dumplings, sauces, omelettes – and a dizzying array of pastries, cakes and breads.

Meals in Canada are taken at times dictated by the common work schedule. The size of break-

❝ Canadians invest much creativity in the potato theme. ❞

fast depends on time and occupation, but generally consists of cereal at least, if not more – eggs done to order, bacon and/or sausages, hash browns (cubed fried potatoes), and, for the really ravenous, pancakes with maple syrup and butter.

The lunch hour begins at 12 o'clock sharp and is usually fairly light, with sandwiches (a popular carry-over from elementary school) or anything that can be partaken of quickly during the midday break, whether you are seated in a packed downtown restaurant or high above a sea of corn in the air-conditioned, computerised cabin of a giant harvester.

The main meal of the day is served punctually at six (or sometimes as early as five on the farm). Nearly all Canadian dinners include potatoes in some form or another, and only occasionally will they be replaced by more exotic fare like noodles or rice. Canadians invest much creativity in the potato theme. Potatoes may be boiled, whipped, scalloped, fried, mashed, sliced, diced, cubed, hashed, or combined with water and flour and rolled into dumplings (a procedure which takes hours, the end product of which is remarkably similar in shape and taste to how they were when they started). Norwegian Canadians even use potatoes to make a seasonal dessert called *lefse*, which consists of potato pastries of crêpe-like thinness spiced with sugar and cinnamon.

> **"Maple syrup is as highly coveted each spring as Beaujolais Nouveau is in France in autumn."**

In what might well be described as their revenge, the Quebecois invented *poutine*. This is basically potatoes – French fries dripping with gravy, special sauce, and (most importantly) cheese curds. Sometimes ketchup is thrown into the mixture for good measure, thus eradicating the possibility of ingesting the mess with any degree of grace whatsoever.

It's a sticky business

Canada is famous for its maple syrup which is a major export and is as highly coveted each spring as Beaujolais Nouveau is in France in autumn.

The syrup is a universal topping – it goes with anything, from ice cream to waffles, rice pudding to toast. Mostly it's used in cooking and baking in lieu of sugar. A much healthier alternative, it's amazing the difference a few drops of pure maple syrup will make to a *ragoût*, a fruit pie, or a cup of hot chocolate.

All over Eastern Canada where most of the sugar maples grow, you can walk into maple woods and see huge trees with sap taps sticking out of them, and sometimes pipes attached to the taps all leading to a small building where the sap is

> **66 Sugar shacks are the châteaux of the Canadian forests. 99**

collected. These sugar shacks, as they are called, are the châteaux of the Canadian forests, and are often large enough to hold social gatherings, with hearty meals, maple syrup tasting, a lively sense of community, endless conversation, singing, fiddling, dancing, and couples slipping away for intimate walks in the moonlit snow, all in the middle of nowhere, but still very close to home.

Systems

Infrastructure

Canada is essentially a horizontal country. (The northern two-thirds of the land, being underdeveloped and underpopulated, are largely ignored.) The Trans-Canada highway is the country's spinal cord, a route that connects the Atlantic Ocean to the Pacific and took 15 years to build.

Two trans-national railways also cross the land,

often sharing the same route but on different sides of the valleys in natural bottlenecks such as the Rocky Mountains. The first railway, completed in 1885, opened up the West to settlers, gold-seekers, and eco-tourists. For instance, in 1881 Manitoba had 10,000 farms, by 1891 there were 55,000, and by 1911, some 200,000.

All Canadians, young and old, thrill to the lonely sound of a distant train horn at night. Nothing except for an NHL winning goal will bring a tear to the eye of the most hardened Canadian male more readily than this haunting sound.

> **66 All Canadians, young and old, thrill to the lonely sound of a distant train horn at night. 99**

The major exception to the horizontal rule is the Alaska Highway in the West. Built by the American military to enable the defence of Alaska against possible Japanese invasion during the Second World War, it was agreed that America would pay for its construction and leave Canada with the maintenance costs. (Ah Canada! Ten months of winter and two months of road repairs.)

Public transportation even within cities is often woefully inadequate, so parents are bombarded with requests for the use of the family vehicle. In most provinces in Canada you can legally drive on your own at 16. This rite of passage comes none too soon for beleaguered parents tired of shuttling their young to and from where they need to go, and it begins a new era in the parent-child relationship, commonly known as the Daddy-can-I-borrow-the-car-Friday-night? phase. Of course, most families have two vehicles, one for each parent, so the most common phrase in any household with a 16-year-old is 'Ask your mother'.

Dealing with the snow

Canadians are used to getting snow – a lot of snow – each winter, and are always well prepared for it. No amount of precipitation brings the nation to a grinding halt. It's no wonder they laugh heartlessly when they hear how 2 cm of snow has incapacitated New York or London (England). Citizens of London, Ontario, wouldn't bat an eye at a snowfall of less than a metre, so news like this makes Canadians temporarily feel superior.

If the snowfall is heavy enough, the otherwise quiet streets resound to the noise of engines whining and tyres

> **66 They laugh heartlessly when they hear how 2 cm of snow has incapacitated New York or London. 99**

spinning on slippery surfaces. The sense of community is reinforced when neighbours need each other's assistance, and it is not uncommon for people to don jackets and mitts without being asked at the sound of a fellow citizen struggling to free his vehicle from the vice-like grip of ice.

When a big freeze is forecast, car owners connect the block heater to the car overnight. Forgetting to plug in might mean it not starting in the morning – and perhaps not until spring. One must take care to observe the schedule when the streets are being cleared. Failure to move your car in timely fashion will result in a fate worse than ticketing or towing; it will quite literally be buried. Nor are cars the only thing one has to keep a lookout for. People in Sault St. Marie are required by law to ensure that their kids are off the streets when the snowblowers go by. Small children have been known to disappear entirely in the ensuing urban avalanche.

> **❝ Failure to move your car in timely fashion will result in a fate worse than ticketing or towing; it will quite literally be buried. ❞**

Canada post

Postage within Canada is set at the same rate, whether the mail is going just down the street or crossing the country, the government thus subsidizing significantly the cost of deliveries to the north and more remote areas. The pick-up and delivery of mail across such a huge country in any weather is quite a feat.

Canada Post also copes with mail for Santa Claus. Over one million letters are handled each year, some with Santa's very own postal code – H0H 0H0. Santa endeavours to respond to every one of them (with some voluntary help from Canada Post employees), taking care, of course, to avoid the public relations disaster that would result in the same form letter being delivered to two children in the same house.

Here's to your health

Statistics show that in Canada women can expect to live 81.3 years, men 4.5 years less. Only residents of Andorra, Macau, and Japan could expect to live much longer.

Each province and territory operates its own compulsory health care system through the tax of its citizens, and the feder-

> **Each province and territory operates its own compulsory health care system.**

al government contributes with transfer payments to the provinces. Cutbacks have been necessary to keep costs within income, and hospitals nationwide are short of nurses, but Medicare, Canada's cradle-to-grave insurance of the health of its citizens, ensures that health care is still of exceptional quality.

Canadian emergency wards tend to be less busy than their American or British counterparts, if only because gunshot wounds and stabbings are a monthly, rather than hourly, occurrence. The exception is the first day of snow, when emergency services are stretched to the limit with the whiplashes and fender-benders (as well as more serious injuries) of motorists who procrastinated just a bit too long before changing over to winter tyres.

Each winter sees a case of serious frostbite, sometimes from among the homeless, very occasionally from among the members of the Polar Bear Club.

Education

Systems across the board

A particular quirk of Canadian education is that there isn't one system but 13. All 10 provinces and all three

> **66 All 10 provinces and all three territories have the right to run their own education systems. 99**

territories have the right to run their own education systems. This is true for the professions as well, and it is frustrating to spend 8 years studying to be a doctor or a lawyer only to find that changing provinces may require yet further training.

More confusing still, 'public' schools are for everybody, while 'separate' schools are entrenched in law as having to exist for Roman Catholics only – a remnant from the days when Canada was intended to be a French-speaking colony with its own language, religion and culture guaranteed. This may overlap with, but is not the same as, the separate/public school system. Thus in some places there may be four separate school boards, divided along religious and linguistic lines: French Catholic, English Catholic, French public and English public.

If all this still does not present you with enough options, you could opt for a private school which will charge tuition fees to educate your child, and then there are public schools with special programmes for exceptionally talented or gifted students. In addition, there is the French Immersion system, popular amongst anglophones, under which English children are sent to school to study and speak in French only, with draconian language laws enforced even on the playground at break.

Having so many different types of schools (private, public, immersion, church and charter) and four different school boards under 13 different

66 Relocating families often get a nasty surprise when they are informed that the children will have to repeat a grade. **99**

departments of education, means there is no national standard. Nobody agrees on the grade at which one makes the transition from elementary to secondary school, nor on how many years' schooling is mandatory, nor how many grades there should be before college or university. Relocating families can get a nasty surprise when they are informed that the children will have to repeat a grade because the one they have just finished does not cover the required syllabus to pass into the next grade where they are now.

Older children from isolated areas may be sent away to boarding schools, but this practice is falling out of favour. These days children in a very small community are more likely to attend the same school from kindergarten to grade 12 (11 in Quebec). In rural areas, pupils are taken to the nearest school in large yellow school buses, some spending over an hour on the bus each way. Stops are tailored to drop off the children at their own driveway. Some never do a spot of homework at home because they always complete it on the bus. Having to catch the bus also provides an excellent excuse for avoiding detention.

> **66 Having to catch the bus also provides an excuse for avoiding detention. 99**

With the advent of computers, high-quality education has now become possible even in very remote areas. It also enables parents (often of stricter religious minorities) to educate their children at home. What these home-schooled kids lose in social upbringing it is believed they gain by avoiding the corrupting influences of contemporary society and an intentionally secular education. Or bigger kids stealing their lunch.

Up to a degree

Fully 75% of Canadian students go on after high school to some sort of further education. Colleges in

Canada are subsidised by provincial government, and consequently, while not free, are a great deal cheaper than anything Stateside, a fact lost on Canadian students who protest vociferously each time tuition fees are raised. Having a university degree is fast becoming the minimum standard for employment but is far from a guarantee of a good job; those with a PhD in Philosophy if not holding tenure at a university are likely to be flipping burgers at the local fast-food joint.

Culture (or lack thereof)

As a collection of immigrants from every country in the world, Canadians are engaged in a constant struggle to share the best and leave the rest, to come up with something greater than the sum of its parts, a conglomerate of cultures that they can appropriate and call their own. In the meantime, what culture they have is imported from elsewhere:

66 What culture Canadians have is imported from elsewhere. 99

for English-speaking Canadians high culture tends to be anything that comes from Europe and popular culture is anything that comes from America. For French-speaking Canadians, French culture imbues them with a casual sense of relaxation, a *joie de vivre*, and a *camaraderie* that can make English Canadians openly envious.

Despite their renown, institutions like the Royal Winnipeg Ballet and the Montreal Symphony Orchestra are largely reliant on government support. Even Montreal's famous circus troupe, Cirque du Soleil, has trouble attracting sufficient funds through audience attendance (except in Las Vegas). The average Canadian citizen's idea of an ideal Friday night is more likely to be a double-header hockey game, three friends, and a 'two-four' (the nickname for a case of beer containing 24 bottles). Culture to most Canadians is not to be found close to the heart but growing between the toes.

> **66 The average Canadian citizen's idea of an ideal Friday night is more likely to be a double-header hockey game. 99**

Prelude to invasion

Because of their proximity to one another, Canadian and American cultures are hopelessly intertwined. It's a recurrent theme in the Canadian mind-set that anything good, successful or popular will promptly be appropriated by the Americans. Basketball as a sport was invented by a Canadian, James Naismith. Canadians founded Warner Bros and produced Mary Pickford, the star of the silent film era, subsequently tagged 'America's sweetheart'.

The annexation of Canada was official American policy which lasted for over 150 years until 1923, since when, to the Canadian eye, the American domination of Canada has merely switched tactics from military to cultural assimilation. Continual cultural incursions have made Canadians defensive to the point where they have taken steps to regulate it. Part of what props up Canadian culture and prevents it from being swallowed up, bought out, or undersold by the American mega-market are the Canadian content laws imposed on the Canadian media. Television (particularly the Canadian Broadcasting Corporation) and radio are required to have a minimum of 30% Canadian content in their programmes.

What constitutes 'Can-con' may be a bit hard to define. Being written, filmed, edited and produced in Canada by Canadians with Canadian actors for Canadian audiences might be overdoing it, but an American company that shoots one scene just inside the Canadian border on a pit stop to Europe will not quite make the grade, not even if the lead actress has a Canadian cousin, three-quarters of the crew have heard of Canada, and the script includes an 'Eh?'.

> **" Television and radio are required to have a minimum of 30% Canadian content in their programmes. "**

Canadians export some of their greatest talent to the States. A list of Canadian movie stars reads almost like a Who's Who of Hollywood: Donald Sutherland, Dan Aykroyd, Christopher Plummer, John Candy, Howie

Mandel, Pamela Anderson, Mike Myers, Leslie Nielsen, Jason Priestley, Keanu Reeves, Brendan Fraser, Hayden Christensen, Monty Hall, Neve Campbell, Michael J. Fox, Jim Carrey, and from *Star Trek*: Captain Kirk and Scottie. If you want to know who is Canadian and who is not, don't ask an American. They can hardly tell the difference. But Canadians just know. It's in their genetic code.

Literature

Canadian literature is dominated by weather and geography which plays out repeatedly in 'survival' themes. Robert Service's early poems of the Yukon have influenced generations with their images of Canada, the land that he called 'all lure, and virgin vastitude'. His action-packed poems of life in the far north have left an indelible impression of a Canada replete with hardy folk battling against extreme conditions (and often losing), and selfless heroes sacrificing themselves to save others' lives.

> 66 Service's poems have left an indelible impression of a Canada replete with hardy folk battling against extreme conditions. 99

Canadians consider Earle Birney's poem, 'David', to be the literary equivalent of Michaelangelo's masterpiece. A narrative in strict pentameter, it tells of two young mountaineers taking advantage of the Canadian

60

wilderness and climbing unscaled heights. The climax of the poem is when one of the two falls, basically due to the fault of the other, and doesn't die, but breaks his back and lies paralysed, perched on the edge of a high precipice. Knowing how long it will take to get help, waiting alone and dreading the life he could be reduced to if he were to survive, he asks his companion to throw him over the ledge.

> **Anne of Green Gables ensures that Prince Edward Island has never suffered from a lack of tourists.**

Every once in a while, Canadian novelists will come up with a bestseller which propels them to international fame: W.O. Mitchell's *Who Has Seen the Wind*, Robertson Davies' *Fifth Business*, and Michael Ondaatje's *The English Patient* are only three examples. Margaret Atwood first gained notoriety for *The Handmaid's Tale*, subsequently the subject of a film and an opera. But none of these match the enduring popularity of Lucy Maude Montgomery's first novel, *Anne of Green Gables*, published in 1908, which ensures that the province of Prince Edward Island has never suffered from a lack of tourists, especially the Japanese who visit Charlottetown each summer in droves.

Children's bedtime reading includes the English classic *Winnie the Pooh* whose name was inspired by a Canadian bear named after Winnipeg (the capital of Manitoba) who became a fixture at London Zoo.

French Canadian literature (which to anglophones means any Canadian literature written in French, whereas in Quebec the term refers specifically to anything written outside Quebec by Canadian French-speakers) is also preoccupied with adversity and survival, but with its own twist. Quebecois literature has traditionally been marked by a sense of struggling to survive, not just against the elements, or against foreign invasions (the Americans were successfully repelled in the Revolutionary War and again in the War of 1812), but in politics. It has been a common theme since the first works of Lionel Groulx in the early 1900s right up to the modern poetry of Paul Chamberland who continues to stress the 'savage need for liberation'.

> **While English Canadian literature might bemoan the lack of a coherent culture, Quebecois literature is more likely to celebrate its own.**

Other writers push boundaries of a different kind: Marie-Claire Blais was a pioneer of the poem-novel, while Roch Carrier's most famous work has a bilingual title: *La Guerre, Yes Sir!* Playwright-turned-novelist Michel Tremblay's works are largely incomprehensible to many excellent French speakers because of the very particular *joual* (Quebecois slang) he uses to speak to the Quebecois in their own voice.

Thus, while English Canadian literature might bemoan the lack of a coherent culture, Quebecois literature is more likely to celebrate its own. Particularly well loved are the singer-songwriters. One such *chansonnier* is Gilles Vigneault, whose song *Gens du Pays* has become the unofficial anthem of Quebec. Equally famous is his *Mon Pays* with its opening line: *Mon pays, ce n'est pas un pays, c'est l'hiver!*, My country is not a country, it's winter. Or, more loosely interpreted: 'I'm cold, therefore I am.'

Song

Folk songs are almost exclusively Maritime (such as *I'se The Bye That Builds The Boat*, which is how Newfies say 'I'm the man!') or French Canadian such as *At The Clear Fountain* and *Ah! If My Monk Would Like To Dance*, which are well known because the Quebecois actually sing them.

While Canadians are proud of their homegrown talents Oscar Peterson, Glenn Gould, Leonard Cohen and Joni Mitchell (who has been honoured with a postage stamp), they are rather more reticent about superstars like Céline Dion. If you are too successful, particularly outside the country, Canadians tend not to like it. It is part of their distaste for showiness. As someone remarked, 'If you win international recognition, the last instrument you should toot is your own horn.'

> **❝ If you are too successful, particularly outside the country, Canadians tend not to like it. ❞**

Cinema

Despite Canadian ownership of Universal Studios, the cinematic scene in Canada remains relatively small, but not insignificant. Vancouver's thriving film industry is referred to by many in the business as 'Hollywood North'.

Denys Arcand is an internationally respected director from Quebec who created such gems as *Jesus of Montreal* and *The Decline of the American Empire* (a subject close to many Canadian hearts). Jean-Claude Lauzon would likely still be shocking Quebecois society with successors to movies such as *Un Zoo la Nuit* and *Léolo* if he hadn't died in a plane crash in 1997. Unfortunately, Canadian films and directors tend to do better at Cannes than they do at the box office, even at home. Exceptions to this are James Cameron (of *Titanic* and *Avatar* fame) and David Cronenberg (*Crash* and *Naked Lunch*) who have become household names.

> **❝ Canadian films and directors tend to do better at Cannes than they do at the box office. ❞**

Many American films are shot in Canada since Canada offers some of the last unspoilt locations in the world. In order to get Canadian cities to pass for American ones, directors often need only change the odd detail, such as splattering litter and graffiti arbitrarily over the set, to make things look more American.

Art

Much of the nation's art takes its inspiration from nature. Inuit soapstone carvings and work by First Nations and Métis fetch increasingly large sums. Michael Snow's sculpture 'Flightstop' in Toronto's Eaton Centre depicting a flock of Canada geese frozen in flight is a powerful example of Canadian creativity.

The Canadian painting scene may never recover from its zenith of the 1920s when the so-called Group of Seven made international headlines in the art world by abandoning the classical form of landscape painting for a vivid and subjective style of self-expression that initially

> 66 Only in Saskatchewan does one have the uninterrupted inspiration, and opportunity, to make a subject of the sky. 99

appalled the art critics. Emily Carr, their contemporary, espoused her own version of impressionism to earn a place in the history of Canadian art.

The works of artists such as Alex Colville and Christopher Pratt still shock audiences with their austere aesthetic of everyday scenes; minimalist Douglas Haynes' canvases feature Rothkoesque squares. Myles McDonald, from Saskatchewan, has made his name painting skyscapes, virtually defining the genre. Land, sea and cityscapes have been painted since time began, but only in Saskatchewan does one have the uninterrupted inspiration, and opportunity, to make a subject of the sky.

The press

Canada has two national papers, *The Globe and Mail* and *The National Post*, both of which have printing centres strategically located across the country to assist in distribution. Headlines might be identical, but advertising and editorial content is intentionally regional, making for different editions depending on where you buy the paper, as well as ensuring a lack of consistent Canadian opinion and shoring up Canadian regionalism.

Where an international news item is being covered, Canadian papers will often include a sidebar which gives a local reaction by people who come from, or whose forebears came from, the area where the event described is taking place. An article on heightened tensions between Pakistan and India will include

66 Headlines might be identical, but advertising and editorial content is intentionally regional. 99

the ravings of the Indian foreign affairs minister and the rantings of the Pakistani response, but printed alongside this you will find a report on how well Indians and Pakistanis are getting along (in true Canadian fashion) in the Centre for Asian Expatriates downtown. Accompanying articles on the situation in Iraq will be a local Iraqi's reaction to the events 'back home'. In whatever country a major event occurs, an impression can always be had from someone near at hand who comes from 'over there'.

Sense of Humour

If other nationalities tend to see the Canadian sense of humour as dry and rather underdeveloped, Canadians merely retort that they haven't appreciated its more intricate subtleties. Like that shown in a favourite joke that goes something like this: 'Ask me if I'm a doctor.' 'Are you a doctor?' 'No.' The irony in the realization that these jokes are not funny is apt to send the average Canadian into gales of laughter.

Lampoons such as *Little Mosque on the Prairie*, and candid camera-type TV spin-offs from the *Juste pour rire* (*Just for Laughs*) festival continue to amuse. *This Hour Has 22 Minutes* (a jibe at the length of the programme minus the commercials) has a sophisticated mix of chat and sketch that regularly attracts Canadian MPs. It is said that some only want to get elected in order to make a guest appearance.

Satirical and ironic, the Canadian sense of humour has gone searching for a subject and, when combined with the genuine Canadian respect for other cultures and general level of politeness, has landed on the only subject that Canadians can safely make fun of with impunity: themselves. A good deal of humour stems from the Canadian genius for compromise which results in many situations where two people, faced with a choice, rather than do either, will do something quite else that neither likes at all.

They also enjoy digs at their neighbour, such as, 'Living next door to the U.S. is like living next door to an alcoholic family. You wave at them every day, and hope they don't come over.'

Custom & Tradition

Canadian families celebrate many traditions brought from their lands of origin; one will observe Yom Kippur, another will organise a funeral wake, those of Ukrainian extraction will wait until 6 January to celebrate Christmas, and Danish Canadians will mark St. Hans on the evening of 23 June with a bonfire on which they burn a witch (only in effigy, fortunately).

The nation enjoys a number of statutory holidays (conveniently timed at approximately one per month).

> **The nation enjoys a number of statutory holidays, conveniently timed at approximately one per month.**

Victoria Day (Canadians are quite happy to have a vacation in honour of the long-gone British royal) is celebrated on the weekend closest to May 24th – expressed as May 'two-four' – and many provincial parks are designated 'alcohol free' on this weekend. It is also the traditional time to open the summer cottage, which is less a desire to escape the heat (rare this early) than to reconnect with the land and the myth that all

Canadians are, or were, pioneers.

Canada Day (1 July) celebrating the nation's found-ing in 1867 gets a slight jump on the Americans with fun and fireworks countrywide, even in Quebec where the festivities are slightly muted (although the Quebecois are by no means so fiercely independent as to refuse to take the day off). In Quebec, Canada Day is eclipsed by the Fête Nationale (24 June) or Fête de Saint Jean Baptiste, the patron saint of Quebec, when there are parades, concerts and local community events and the streets in Quebec City and Montreal are festooned with blue fleur-de-lis.

> **Because in Quebec all leases expire at the end of June, Canada Day has become Moving Day.**

The Quebecois have long made special use of 1st July. Because in Quebec all leases expire at the end of June, Canada Day has become Moving Day. It is the one day in the year when in Montreal you cannot rent a truck unless it has been reserved since December, and no-one knows a single soul with a truck or van who isn't either busy helping someone else, or wisely being out of town. It's a nightmare for students and low renters. Of course the people moving into the place you're vacating arrive before your truck does, so you move all your furniture on to the lawn, only to discover that at the new place all you can do is to camp on the lawn because their truck hasn't arrived yet (in fact, they booked the same truck you did and need you to empty it so they can start to load).

Labour Day, in September, provides a last chance for people to get away before the school year begins, and to winterproof the cottage. Thanksgiving is celebrated on the second weekend in October, well in advance of the American one. Corn, beans and squash (named 'the three sisters' by the Iroquois to whom they were the physical and spiritual sustainers of life), turkey, pumpkin (made into a pie) and other vegetables that the native people showed the settlers how to grow to avoid starvation, are features of this fête.

> **" Labour Day provides a last chance for people to winterproof the cottage. "**

Although Thanksgiving is not strictly a religious festival, churches are massively decorated with cornucopias overflowing with autumn fruits and foods and lavishly arrayed with the bright Canadian autumn leaves of reds and golden yellow. It is a testament to survival in a harsh climate, and is one of the most heavily attended church services of the year.

Remembrance Day on 11 November is the opportunity for another day off if you skip the memorial service at the local Royal Canadian Legion. But then you would miss the reading of *In Flanders Fields*, the famous war poem written by Canadian John McCrea when serving as a medical officer in the First World War: 'In Flanders fields the poppies blow/Between the crosses, row on row ...'

Industry & Business

Working like a beaver

The shy and hardworking beaver provides an admirable role model for how best to handle the winter: construct elaborate warm houses to cope with the cold, then stay indoors. The evolutionary development of Canadians is the addition of satellite television and a 'two-four'.

Like the beaver, they work hard. Most of the population is descended from people who decided to leave home for a largely unknown destination, the kind

> **The first to brave the wilds were certainly not the illuminati and academics of Europe, but hardy stock.**

who were lured by untamed wilderness. The first to brave the wilds were certainly not the illuminati and academics of Europe, but hardy stock, and it still shows, from survivalist attitudes to the Protestant work ethic.

An aptitude for hard physical work is evident in the significant numbers of Canadians who are employed in primary industries like steel, mining, oil and timber. Over 100,000 people are employed in forestry either indirectly (replanting, growing, hauling, administration) or directly (chainsawing and 'skidding' – dragging the cut timber out of the forest). Formerly, rivers were used to transport timber. Log drivers rode the river on the logs recovering caught-up stragglers and breaking up log jams. Canadian television, to increase its

'Can-con', used to intersperse commercials with *The Log Driver's Waltz*, a folk song now heavily engrained in the hearts and minds of many Canadians.

Although some people still make their living by hunting and trapping, there are dwindling numbers of fishermen on both East and West coasts. The over-fishing of the Grand Banks has depleted the stock to such an extent that most Newfoundlanders have had to look for other sources of income. This unfortunate situation for the Newfies is a source of mirth for other Canadians who come up with witty comparisons such as 'What do Newfies and sperm have in common? A million-to-one chance of being employed.'

Confronting the elements is not restricted to rugged outdoorsmen and those living in isolated rural areas. Many Canadians have at one point been employed in distinctly outdoor pursuits. For example, to help pay their tuition fees it is not uncommon among university students to backpack into the 'boondocks' to plant trees or fight fires for the summer, sometimes in areas so remote they are only accessible by helicopter. No matter how hot the sun and how much the sweat runs down your face to mix with several days' grime, no matter if the mosquitoes are so thick that you cannot breathe without inhaling some, no matter how hard it rains or hails or even snows in the middle of spring in the mountains, in Canada you do not complain. To do so would be unCanadian.

Canadian style commerce

Canada is a success story. Its standard of living is comparable to the highest in the world and its economy ranks in the top ten. Though viewed by outsiders as merely a source for raw materials, the nation is in fact a world leader in certain fields, such as computer and iron ore technology.

> **The Mom-and-Pop operations running the town store, gas station or farm have mostly been bought out by big businesses.**

In the past few decades Canadian business has been transformed. The Mom-and-Pop operations running the town store, neighbourhood gas station or farm have mostly been bought out by big businesses that sometimes then employ the former owners to work them. However, the Internet has brought a new age of small businesses competing with the large ones and many long-time employees are electing to become self-employed or take early retirement.

Some executives, disdaining the 'gotta-get-ahead' mentality, say 'no' to overtime and have cut back on their work hours to 'point-eight time' (permanent 3-day weekends) or even half-time, in order to spend more quality time with those who mean the most to them – their families.

Canadian businesses mostly take a fairly relaxed attitude towards dress and on-the-job comportment. Casual Fridays have become commonplace, and at Halloween employees may come to work dressed up as their favourite character, with corporate approval. This is why if you show up on 31 October to negotiate a loan you just might find yourself discussing your credit history with the bank manager masquerading as the devil.

Canada did not have a banking crisis. In 2008 Canada's banking system was ranked the healthiest in the world (the USA being 40th, the UK 44th). Partly this reflects Canada's risk-averse business culture (Canadians refused to follow the US business models), partly that massive over-consumption is not seen as a worthy goal in the pursuit of happiness, and partly just good old mistrust of the USA.

Government

How's your Constitution holding up?

Canada being a constitutional monarchy means that, while still paying lip service to the British crown, the government basically does as it pleases. The Queen is represented in Canada by a Governor General who has two residences, one in Ottawa, the other in Quebec City. A Lt. Governor is also appointed for each province.

The head of the Queen is found on Canadian coinage. The Canadian dollar comes in the form of a coin which is referred to, because of the loon (a water bird) depicted on the flip side, as a 'loonie'. When a bi-metallic two dollar coin was introduced in 1996, it didn't take long to be dubbed a 'toonie'. Local heroes grace the bank notes. This does not mean, however, that anyone will be able to tell you just whose likeness is represented on a given denomination.

Canadians only took home their own Constitution in 1982. Prior to this, changes had to be approved by the House of Lords in Britain and signed by Her Majesty. Gaining the right to make constitutional changes for themselves should have been a triumph, but it caused more problems than it solved. The idea was to have the new Constitution ratified by all ten provinces. It wasn't: Quebec got cold feet and refused to sign. This sparked a constitutional conundrum that has yet to be concluded. Several major attempts have been made to rectify the situation, but Quebec is still not technically within the country's constitutional framework. Everyone ignores this inconvenient fact as much as possible.

> **66** Gaining the right to make constitutional changes for themselves should have been a triumph, but it caused more problems than it solved. **99**

Bureaucracy

The administration of Canada is divided into three levels: federal, provincial, and municipal. This presents the electorate with a dizzying number of elections, and one can almost hear the collective sigh of relief should the country get through an entire year without some campaign going on that responsible citizens feel obliged to follow.

❝ There are 4,200 local municipal governments of which one sixth are called Saint-something-or-other. ❞

Between the federal government in Ottawa, 10 provincial governments, three territorial governments and almost exactly 4,200 local municipal governments (one sixth of which are called Saint-something-or-other), the number of people who work directly or indirectly for the government is roughly a fifth of the Canadian workforce.

At the municipal level, representatives are elected to a local council or city hall, but generally the only people who have any interest in municipal elections are the ones running in them. This is in stark contrast to the rabid campaigns fought for positions on school boards, where nothing less than the future of the children and therefore the entire nation is at stake.

From the tax forms Canadians are required to fill out annually to the occasional Royal Commission investigation into behaviour that somebody has considered scandalous, governance in Canada generates mountains of paper – in duplicate, for everything published in one language must be done in the other. It's a good thing there are plenty of trees.

Politics

Canadian author Pierre Berton once boasted that a Canadian is 'someone who knows how to make love in a canoe'. Those in the know confirm that making love in a canoe is distinctly precarious since it requires making waves without rocking the boat. The balance between these two is the fine line that Canadian politics likes to tread.

For a long time politics have been a contest between the liberal and conservative elements of society with government almost perfectly alternating between the two political parties with those names. The New Democratic Party (NDP), which is the most left-leaning, had until the 2011 federal election historically always come third, but they nonetheless retain a healthy inferiority complex that is thoroughly Canadian.

If you don't care for these, just vote for one of the many 'fringe' parties in Canada. You can opt for the Communist party, or the Canadian Clean Start Party (who would like to confiscate all private property to abrogate the national debt). The Marijuana Party's main plank is the legalization of the weed (might as well, some say, as it's found in just about every farmer's field), and the Natural Law Party advocates spreading the 'influence of coherence' through 'communal Yogic Flying'.

> **66** Author Pierre Berton once boasted that a Canadian is 'someone who knows how to make love in a canoe'. **99**

Canada's six time zones have an interesting effect on the running of elections. On polling day the lights are out on the victor's celebration in the East long before the last of the votes from the West have been tallied. Because of this, results used to be withheld. Even if the winner was known, the news was blacked out until all the polling stations had closed, and the results were only made public nationally on the 10 o'clock news that night (10.30 in Newfoundland). But the prospect of prosecuting every Internet user who transgressed this rule put paid to this embargo.

> **66 On polling day the lights are out on the victor's celebration in the East long before the last of the votes from the West have been tallied. 99**

Canadian elections are not fixed to some predetermined timeline (as are, for example, American presidential elections, occurring in November every four years), and their variability can add to the constant bracing of the electorate. Will we have another election this year? Will the Christmas season be blighted by a campaign season?

Defence

Only three people per square kilometre but more land to defend than any other country except Russia means that keeping the 'True North Strong and Free' (as the national anthem has it) could be an impossibly demanding task. Luckily, the Canadians have the climate working for them: invading armies from the north would be less likely to require a military response than a search and rescue.

Another part of Canada's defence systems is CSIS (pronounced 'seesis') – the Canadian Security Intelligence Service, a secret service so secret that even some Canadians don't know about it.

Canada's military forces are involved in just about every UN peace-keeping operation, but without conscription they are hard-pressed to find sufficient recruits to maintain the 50,000-odd personnel that they have. However, Canada's ultimate defence plan lies not in the strength of its army, navy and airforce, but in letting the Americans take care of any menace. Passing on all defence costs to your neighbour is an economical way of being able to tackle

> **Canadians have the climate working for them: invading armies would be less likely to require a military response than a search and rescue.**

much more important issues (like who's going to win the Stanley Cup). It also frees up young men to do more constructive things with their time, like play hockey.

If the Yanks ever attack Canada, then there's not much that the Canadians will be able to do about it. But they have a plan in the event of that happening:

welcome them in like the neighbours they are, get them floor-licking drunk on some half-decent beer (for a change), and then clobber them with hockey sticks. It's one weapon that all Canadian households are sure to have.

Law & Order

Canadian law is based on British law. Quebec though, has its own civil law, so in that province both traditions are in effect with the happy result for lawyers that one might be required to pay even more money to sort it out – particularly if one is unilingual.

First Nations feel that Canadians have always helped where they are concerned – helped themselves, that is, to their land, their resources, their culture, their language and their identity. In fact Canadians 'helped' the native people so much that only in 2011 did First Nations people on reserves gain the same human rights as other Canadians.

The high level of bureaucracy in Canada applies to Canadian law as well. It is estimated that there are 40,000 laws (not including municipal bylaws) by which the conscientious citizen must abide, and of which ignorance is no excuse. For example, in accordance with some archaic laws, children in Calgary are required to obtain the permission of the mayor before engaging in a snowball fight; Edmonton cyclists are expected to use hand signals before making a turn while conscientiously keeping both hands on the handlebars at all times; Saskatoon has outlawed attempting to catch fish with your hands, and misdemeanours in Ottawa include eating ice-cream cones in public on the Sabbath.

The Mounties

In a survey of 11 Western industrialized countries, Canada has the highest percentage of people (80%) who believe their police are effective in controlling crime – this despite having the third lowest number of officers per 100,000 population. This has to be due in no small measure to the fame of their national icon, the Mounties – the Royal Canadian Mounted Police, or *Gendarmerie Royale*.

Other than in Ontario and Quebec (who have their own provincial police force), the RCMP are contracted by every province to enforce the law outside the municipalities. Within city boundaries, local police forces keep you on the straight and narrow. This demarcation, however, is more generally than legalistically observed, so it will do you no good to race at full speed towards the city limits in order to

66 Canada has the highest percentage of people (80%) who believe their police are effective. 99

outrun the RCMP's jurisdiction: your appeal will be laughed out of court.

The Mountie presents a public persona of honesty, integrity, politeness and fairness that is the hallmark of Canadian virtue, an image that is protected by the Mounted Police Foundation through selective approval of the use of Mountie paraphernalia, royalties from which are channelled into community projects all over the country. Thus permission needs to be obtained to reproduce their snazzy red serge outfits which, contrary to the impression given in the movies, are not worn every day but largely reserved for ceremonial events and escorting various dignitaries.

> **The Mountie image is protected through selective approval of the use of Mountie paraphernalia.**

So revered is this uniquely Canadian force that there was a huge furore when a Sikh cadet requested permission to wear his turban, as required by his religion, instead of the RCMP hat. The case went to court and was debated intensely by every newspaper editor and bar patron in the land. In the end it was agreed that the Mounties' uniform could not be held to be more important than the rights and freedoms the wearers of that uniform are sworn to protect. Canadian culture survived the wreckage and the sun still set that night, but just barely, according to some.

Language

Many Canadian contributions to the English and French language are derived from the native Canadian culture which was in place before the arrival of Europeans. Words like 'igloo' and 'parka' and 'mukluk' (moccasins made from leather or seal-hide) are legacies of the Inuit in the north, while the Plains tribes gave 'chinook' (a fleeting but warm winter wind coming from the mountains), 'wigwam' and 'teepee' (portable conical housing), and the Algonqian 'moccasin' and 'toboggan'. Most of these words are centred on a wintry theme. The Inuit have over 40 words for snow.

> **Someone might be described as 'so handy he could fix the crack of dawn'.**

Canadians have also contributed a huge variety of metaphorical expressions. Some are merely variations on the well-known; for example, it's not 'hotter than hell', it's 'hotter than a whore's doorknob on payday'. She can't 'talk the hind leg off a horse' as much as she can 'talk the ears off a corn stalk'. Others are original: someone might be described as 'dumber than a box of hair' or, 'so handy he could fix the crack of dawn' or, 'about as handsome as the south end of a northbound cow'. Some have to do with the weather: 'It was so dry this summer in southern Alberta that the trees got up and went looking for the dogs.'

Vive la différence

Being a minority language in a sea of English in North America, French has required some reinforcement to prevent it being overwhelmed. A unique language regulation, Bill 101, made it illegal for businesses in Quebec to display signs outdoors in any language other than French. Enforcing this law is the language police who patrol streets and byways zealously looking for foreign incursions. An early-morning

> **66** French has required some reinforcement to prevent it being overwhelmed. **99**

raid was made on a doughnut franchise where some 15,000 'offensive' paper bags labelled 'Dunkin' Donuts' were confiscated because they did not include a French translation of the label (never mind the fact that they were written in questionable English to begin with).

This not unreasonable paranoia about preserving the language has led to a few amusing scenarios. Whereas a Frenchman might be content to accede, at least popularly, to '*le hot dog*', a Quebecois, out of deference to Bill 101, gives it the most French sound-ing name possible: '*le chien chaud*'.

Some Canadian French evolved from English, like '*bécosse*', the Quebec word for 'outhouse', which is said to come from the phrase 'in [the] back of the house'. The term 'Mush!', a command for dogs to start pulling the sled, is believed to derive from the

French '*Marche!*' While most English swearwords are sexual in origin, Quebecois curses generally profane the Catholic church.

In Quebec most films and TV programmes in English are dubbed into Quebec French (with an international French accent for ease of comprehension and regional neutrality). Occasionally, the dubbing of a series or a movie, such as *The Simpsons*, is made using the more widely-spoken *joual* variety of Quebec French. This has the advantage of making children's films and TV series comprehensible to younger audiences, but many bi-lingual Quebecois would prefer subtitles since they would then understand some or all of the original audio.

> **In Quebec most films and TV programmes in English are dubbed into Quebec French.**

Linguists come from France to study the language spoken in the remote area of northern Quebec because it is closest to French as spoken in late medieval times. Today's Canadian French differs from French French in accent and terminology. Given time, however, most visitors from France could acclimatise to the strong Quebec accent since they are used to hearing plenty of varieties at home – from Marseilles to Montmartre. But anything less than a fortnight, and a Frenchman from Gascogne speaking with a Canadian from Gaspé might have an easier time if they communicate in English.

The Authors

The son of two pastors, **Vaughn Roste** grew up on the prairies of Alberta's Bible Belt and in the mountains of BC. He also lived for a while on a dairy farm in Quebec, where he quickly realized that he didn't speak French nearly as well as the Canadian educational system had lead him to believe that he did.

A career, nearly a decade long, of living in a tent every summer and planting trees acquainted him all too well with Canada's wilderness and wild life.

It also enabled him to pay for three degrees (one in theology and two in music) and to explore his own and other nations. His travels, often on government or church sponsored programmes, have taken him through the United States and Europe and on to Israel, Colombia, El Salvador, Australia and Togo – all the while proudly sporting his maple leaf pin.

He is currently teaching at a university in Oklahoma while completing a doctorate in music at Louisiana State University. He claims that his continuing residency in the United States is part of an ongoing patriotic plan to raise awareness of Canada throughout the world. In fact he does so in order to avoid shovelling the walk.

Peter W. Wilson is a director and arbitrator in a management and labour relations consulting business, married to a Canadian-born British barrister. He was born in the Ottawa area and blossomed over time into the quintessential Canadian always fighting for the underdog.

Having substantially advanced Canadian unity by convincing as many as would listen that the best parts of their culture were whatever they themselves were not – he moved to England. Whilst extolling the virtues of all things Canadian to the British and all things British to the Canadians, he is careful at all times to point out that he is NOT American.

Snow, when it happens, results in his rushing into the nearest park to take photos and to snowshoe. His time is otherwise occupied in a dauntless search for *tortières*, fresh corn on the cob, and someone who can make a pumpkin pie.

The Americans

Americans are friendly because they just can't help it. However a wise traveller realises that a few happy moments with an American do not translate into a permanent commitment of any kind. This is a nation whose most fundamental social relationship is the casual acquaintance.

The Germans

The Germans strongly disapprove of the irrelevant, the flippant, the accidental. On the whole they would prefer to forgo a clever invention rather than admit that creativity is a random and chaotic process.

The English

The English share a dislike of anyone behaving in a manner that 'goes too far'. The admired way to behave in almost all situations is to display a languid indifference. Even in affairs of the heart, it is considered unseemly to show too much enthusiasm.

The Italians

Italians grow up knowing that they have to be economical with the truth. All other Italians are, so if they didn't play the game they would be at a serious disadvantage. They have to fabricate to keep one step ahead.

The Scots

There is an abstract and intellectual quality to the Scots mind that rejoices in uncomfortable thoughts. A true Scot would sooner be right than rich, any time.

The Swedes

The Swedes brood a lot over the meaning of life in a self-absorbed sort of way without ever arriving at satisfactory answers. The stark images and unresolved plots in many Ingmar Bergman films are accurate snapshots of the Swedish psyche.

Comments on other Xenophobe's® Guides

On the series:

'An enlightened new series, good natured, witty and useful. It deserves a real cheer.'

Reviewer of *The European*

The Poles:

'Entertaining, insightful and a lot of fun – it made me laugh out loud!'

Reader from London, UK

The Americans:

'Stunning observations about American culture that not even most Americans would realize are true.'   Reader from Boston, USA

The Aussies:

'A humorous and accurate description of Australians. You won't want to put it down. It's so good that it was used as a study text for immigrants learning English in Oz.'

Reader from Australia

The Danes:

'The true nature of the Danes revealed. This book has a wonderful energetic sense of irony and humour, combined with a deep insight into the Danish culture and mentality.'   Reader from Denmark

Xenophobe's® guides

Available as printed books and e-books:

The Americans	The Kiwis
The Aussies	The Norwegians
The Austrians	The Poles
The Belgians	The Portuguese
The Canadians	The Russians
The Chinese	The Scots
The Czechs	The Spanish
The Danes	The Swedes
The Dutch	The Swiss
The English	The Welsh
The Estonians	
The Finns	
The French	
The Germans	
The Greeks	
The Icelanders	French
The Irish	German
The Israelis	Greek
The Italians	Italian
The Japanese	Spanish

Xenophobe's® lingo learners

French
German
Greek
Italian
Spanish

Xenophobe's Guides

Xenophobe's® Guides e-books are available from Amazon, iBookstore, and other online sources, and via:

www.xenophobes.com

Xenophobe's® Guides print versions can be purchased through online retailers (Amazon, etc.) or via our web site:

www.xenophobes.com

Xenophobe's® Guides are pleased to offer a quantity discount on book orders. Why not embellish an occasion – a wedding goody bag, a conference or other corporate event with our guides. Or treat yourself to a full set of the paperback edition. Ask us for details:

Xenophobe's® Guides

telephone: +44 (0)20 7733 8585
e-mail: info@xenophobes.com

Xenophobe's® Guides enhance your understanding of the people of different nations. Don't miss out – order your next Xenophobe's® Guide soon.

Xenophobe's Guides